LIKE
ANY ROAD
ANYWHERE

D0239398

Other books of poetry
by Ernest Sandeen

Antennae of Silence (1953)

Children and Other Strangers (1961)

LIKE ANY ROAD ANYWHERE: NEW POEMS

193050

ERNEST SANDEEN

PQ 7296
J6L5

UNIVERSITY
OF NOTRE DAME PRESS
NOTRE DAME   LONDON

Copyright © 1976 by
University of Notre Dame Press
Notre Dame, Indiana 46556

The author makes grateful acknowledgment to the editors of the following publications in which these poems first appeared:

Choice: "Watchman, What of the Night?" (© 1962).

Indiana Writes: "Children Lying in the Dazed Heaps of their Bones" (© 1976), "The Way Down" (© 1976).

The Iowa Review: "Celebrants" (© 1971), "Fall Rain" (© 1973), "Light as a Quality of Mercy" (© 1973), "Mountains" (© 1973), "The Poem as a Private Persecutor" (© 1974), "The Poem Dresses Up Like Love" (© 1974), "The Poem Is Showing" (© 1974), "The Poem Out on a Night Mission" (© 1974).

The Minnesota Review: "Evelyn in the April Sun" (© 1969), "Rainy Day: Jogging Indoors" (© 1969).

The New Yorker: "Nearing Winter" (© 1966).

The Ontario Review: "Designs for Sleep" (© 1974), "Dog Drinking at Night" (© 1974).

Poetry: "Day in June" (© 1965), "Growing into Light" (© 1968), "Those Elders of the Great Tradition & the Rest of Us" (© 1968), "Her Poem" (© 1975), "The Poem as Baby-Sitter" (© 1975), "Survival against the Poem" (© 1975).

Poetry Northwest: "What to Do at the End" (© 1969), "In Pursuit" (© 1975).

Prism International: "Love Game" (© 1970), "Organon" (© 1970).

Saturday Review: "Views of Our Sphere" (© 1969), "Suddenly This Left-Handed Life" (© 1970), "Hijack" (© 1970), " 'A Little Folding of the Hands to Sleep' " (© 1971), "The Cricket Sound" (© 1971).

Notre Dame Scholastic: "Diana at Lakeside" (© 1972), "Narcissus Flowering" (© 1972), "Orchestra" (© 1972), "Posture" (© 1974), "Undone, Doing" (© 1974).

Shenandoah: "Nearest of Kin" (© 1970).

Library of Congress Cataloging in Publication Data

Sandeen, Ernest Emanuel, 1908–
  Like any road anywhere.

  I. Title.
PS3537.A6233L5   811'.5'2   76-635
ISBN 0-268-01255-5

Manufactured in the United States of America

FOR EILEEN

These marigolds, petunias, dahlias,
geraniums and daisies are from your planting.
Their reds and yellows wear your modest intensities.

I see your eyes love them below their small bright faces.
Their look tingles down your arms to the roots
you fingered into place in our springtime soil.

Do you know what love it is you were born for?
Your care, the slumbering earth, uses your eyes
to waken to its art of leaf and blossom.

I've loved you for forty years with fingers
that move from love in eyes down to the dark
where our two lives tangle in a root of flesh.

Yet I have merely secrets that I could tell
of you. Your privacies are names as slow as aeons,
they move in verbs too deep, too long for speech.

CONTENTS

1.
ENTER THE POEM

THE POEM OUT ON A NIGHT MISSION

He stands in the abrupt night
of her door, the poem standing
beside him, anxious. With erect
fist he pounds at her wooden
body. Open up, you bitch,
my love, damn you, open
yourself up, you sweet bitch.
(What language for a lover,
grumbles the poem, shivering.)

I've become all instrument,
I'm my only weapon, I've made
myself all key to push myself
whole into your lock, I'll make
you all lock, I'll unlock you.

Faintly the door swings
from its frame (like thighs
spreading, the poem thinks,
remembering her bed the day before).

I have a guest. Won't you come in
and meet him? Slowly he enters
her body with the other man.
The blood of his fist sinks.

Love is a telephone receiver
wrenched off its hook, it drains
drop by drop into an all-night
busy-signal.

                    The poem
disappears behind everything.
Gathering the light of half-moon
and a few stars into its mind
it creates the city end to end.

Across the street there's a weighty matron
looks out her window. What a beautiful
night, she almost whispers, troubled
by an old magic. Of course it's beautiful,
the poem says, but who can know,
if I don't, what it's made of?

THE POEM DRESSES UP LIKE LOVE

The poem contrives to look as old
as love itself, Sappho in Merlin's white beard.
It questions the glum lover: So how did
your story end? I told her I was leaving her.
I couldn't tell her I knew she was leaving
me for her new lover. Your pride, was it?
(Stroking the beard) My pride, yes. And besides
I didn't want her to hurt, even a little.

You ungrateful egotist, mutters the venerable
poem, you could have left her a small gift
of her guilt. What if she wants to remember you?

THE POEM AS A PRIVATE PERSECUTOR

Despair, the poem says to its victim,
was what you wanted from the start.
You wanted the toy, the cloth animal
you'd fondled from childhood to turn
real. You wanted a real lover now
who could enter you live and lash
your blood till your haven of bone
shattered to fragments.

And of course, the poem pontificates,
you found her. She was there
when you looked. (I helped you look.)
Destiny, poem wagging a finger, is nothing
but what your whole life asks for.

Go straight to hell, thinks the victim,
and turns a bare back to the poem
though not so abruptly as to risk whipping.

THE POEM AS BABY-SITTER

I

Her father kisses her cheek,
then slams the car door shut
and the dim light over her head is quenched.
Kiss and dark feel the same to her,
they close her in, alone,
outside her father's voluminous night.

Only the poem stays with her.
The poem, she thinks, is comic books
piled in the back seat.
It's too dark now to read them.

She hears her father's shadow
walking fast on concrete whispers to the house.
She watches. The door blinks open,
stares, winks shut. And father
has disappeared into a woman
standing tall in a blonde moment of light.

Her housecoat was red, the child
records as for a picture not yet composed.
The poem will remember.

II

How willful a girl-child is
who is told to wait. She'll march
on the small feet of her aloneness
toward any forbidden house. And the poem,
the sad reluctant poem, will guide her
to the bedroom window because it must.

The slit in the furry curtain is narrow
but wide enough for a poem's eye of a child.

At first all she sees is tossing nakedness,
a mad comic book not read before,
all men and women in the world naked.
And then wild pictures focus clear to father
wrestling the woman, he pins her
to her bed, flat on her back,
she writhes under him, eyes closed.

The poem hears its girl-child listen
to older brothers as far away as home
cheering for Dad, waving their muscles.

Night air goes sick as fumes,
she gags, trying to breathe,
and the poem huddles her back to the car.
She waits there for her father's wheels
to hurry the whole earth forward.

She shivers, the poem warms her with silence,
it hears her scramble among her selves,
knocking things over.
She's looking for what she barely knows,
like a rumor indistinctly heard on school playgrounds.

She whispers to the poem as to a self:
He's making me again, isn't he,
inside a woman who is not my mother.
Tomorrow I must choose to be reborn
out of the woman's or my mother's strangeness.

SURVIVAL AGAINST THE POEM

The poem sits on the same chair
as the lover. They look like one.
The lover and his love are saying
their last goodbyes by telephone.
Their poem dwindles to lone words,
to whispers, to silence. Reaching out
as for a last caress the lover
lowers the telephone handset gently
down on its bed. It clicks in place
like a heavy lock no one has a key to.

The poem melts from him through the wall.
Outside, it flies up on black wings,
it rests on the telephone line still warm
with the old, the long goodbye of lovers.

The lover can't move in his chair.
Like a shattered web of wires his nerves
let go of him, they let him drop down
the unplumbed hole inside his skin.
Here where belly and guts are blind
animals that jostle him in the dark
and the wet mouths of heart and lungs
softly nuzzle him, he snuggles warm.
Below despair is safer than above.

So sit there on your telephone wire,
old blackbird of a poem, your claws
tingling with the long farewell of lovers.

The lover won't move for you, won't tempt
destruction by a single twitch of thought.
He waits and slowly begins to change
into an ugly, shapeless thing
whose stench rises from a million years
in the sea. He crawls on feeble fin-legs
onto land, into air, he breathes pain
like lightning flashing back at the sun.
Sprawled on his rock he celebrates
as dimly, as dumbly as glands the breathing
that is in him, the thump of blood.

So tickle your toes, dark ode of a bird,
with the sad electric glow of love's long ending.
Ages below you the lover lives.
He grins in the dark like some misshapen fish.

HER POEM

I

The poem is all hers. It begins
with questions: how did she arrive
at this strange place that for thirty
years had always looked like home?

Is her affliction a disease long
undetected or a sudden wound?
She grows thin, sleeps little, her eyes
darken to see ghosts everywhere.

She becomes her own desperate detective,
searching out his car, empty
and still as death, in the woman's driveway.
(No ghost, this, the poem concedes.)

II

Her door cheeps open like a bird
troubled in its nest. He is home.
His false kiss betrays in her a mob
of armed agonies she never knew were there.

This man whose grazing sleeve was enough
to cure all ills goes numb as ice.
Priests of her soul sit hunched around her,
hands on knees like limp clichés.

In the same instant she and the poem
understand: only this Judas,
this familiar stranger, can heal her now.
The one lover she needs is her betrayer.

III

The poem lowers her in a pool of sleep
and there her love is squeezed from her flesh
in a chain of pointed stones. Where
is her Iscariot? Will he kiss her blood?

Winter dawdles. Will spring ever come?
she asks the poem, waking. Will spring
bring back nothing but this: at midday
a mock lover reeling with moonlight?

IV

The earth rolls over on its back
inviting love. The poem points to where
her lover comes weighted with his flagon
of repentant wine. He pours it over

POEM BY MOVIE CAMERA

I

The poem enters your head, takes over your eyes.
You're still yourself, yet now you're the poem's dream
of you. You see, but you don't control the muscles
of your seeing. Else why would you be scanning,
back and forth, the green rug at your feet?
What could you expect to find? Until your gaze
is fixed for you on a brown oak leaf that punctuates
the green current of the floor. Is it a question,
a statement, a command?

              The poem that dreams
your eyes pulls you near. You must obey, you kneel
and the leaf grows larger, larger, filling all you see.
It lies deep in the rug like the fossil footprint
of an animal long extinct.

              The soundtrack
picks up the mellow scuff of footsteps coming close.
And there before you, before the leaf, two soft leather
slippers halt. The camera tilts your eyes up,
slowly, to absorb the figure of a man, inch by inch,
in pyjamas and dressing robe. His hair flows white,
his back is slightly bent, his shoulders slightly stooped.
He's looking down. (But he can't see you of course.
He's real, you're the dream, remember?)

He stoops and from the microphone inside him
you hear the rasp of joints, the thudding swim
of blood to brain. You see a hand of dry skin
and knotted knuckles claw the leaf up like a harvest.

You watch him straighten. He shuffles toward a desk
in the dim corner. In a brief ritual of hands
he crumbles the leaf like fire crackling into an ashtray.

He talks to himself. (He doesn't know you're here, remember?)
He tells himself, It's the one thing I've done today,
picking up an oak-leaf, November-brown,
and so I keep my green floor clear.

II

I wish, the poem says, I could give you
eyes and ears three centuries back.
Because imagine him sitting there
in an upper room of a public house
or in a room next to the stage, actors
pushing in and out to put on costumes, faces.
You hear his quill plop in ink,
jerk across the page in staccato scratches.
A dream-world of queens and wenches,
kings and clowns, flutters down to you
on the feather waving in his fingers.

He's just finished his tragedy of a man
gone wild with the pride of age and grief.
It's all I've done this day, he tells himself,
revising a dozen lines. And I wish you may expire
with every word, you withered bull's pizzle.
(He's thinking of the ancient who plays the king
and has complained about his speeches in the death scene.)

III

It's almost a year later the poem dreams you
again, outdoors at night. You see the camera crew
busy as ghosts under stars that are millions of years
ago. A telescopic lens becomes your eye,
sweeping the milky way, slowly, back and forth.
The crowd of stars leap clear but among them all
not a wisping memory of a man who picks a leaf up
off a floor, who revises a play, who rages in a storm.

The poem's pictures, you protest, fall out from machines
of eyeballs, nerves and brain. They point you to the wrong places.
But you're inside the poem, inside yourself.
You can see. You can even see how far old men and young
can go and where the poem and old and young men end.
You can see, you're inside. In slow motion
you breathe into yourself that indifferent joy
you've always wanted to love with.
You bless the poem with both hands.
Your blessing beams out in all directions.

SLEEPING ON DOWN

Sleeping as you do in a basement
with a sleeping dog is already,
the poem argues, a downward
joining toward origins, a slippage.

To sleep with the fish that are suspended
in the ocean would be a deeper drowning,
and how near the zero of creation
sinks the limp dream the seaweed
is tangled in?

              So be careful,
the poem warns, where you begin
to sleep your nights down from,
especially if your finny fingers
itch to write of such decremental
linkages. After all, says the poem,
I have myself to think of.

THE POEM TAKES A WALK

The greatest thinker of the age walks in the middle.
My father walks on the other side of him.
I'm nearest you, moving in the poem, watching
for you with the poem's eyes.

                         I've forgotten the great man's
name but it doesn't matter, he's known to everyone. He walks
unmindful of his innocence as if strangers had hastily bought
his expensive clothes and flung them around him.

                              Although
my father keeps precisely abreast, it's *his* stride,
easy and bouncy, that leads. His right arm, swinging,
swings the wise man's left, like two arms linked in handcuffs.

I can't believe how freely my father swings
his left hand too, a two-pronged hook of steel,
the weapon which wounded every day of my boyhood
but which he used to hide in his pocket whenever
strangers came to our elm-shaded, half-opened door.

The street we march down feels like the natural dark
between night and morning stretched out unnaturally long.
A few huddled, faceless figures, groping singly, in pairs,
in small groups, must do for people. Occasional cars
float by, glare-eyed blind, rubber-deaf. Streetlamps
fumble the clear air as if lighted by fog.

Dirt farmer, and janitor at last, my father
could not remember which April he quit the one-room school
on the hill where all the twenty pupils ciphered
and read from the same two books year after year.

Now he and the man of wisdom walk together
in bland assurance. I stumble trying to keep in step
with them, my father's left foot timed to the great man's
right. Is it a dance they both were born with?
Or have they rehearsed it many times in a secret place?
I who am known by my father's walk never knew my father.

Maybe where he's been dead for thirty years
my father has learned where he must marshal
the wise man of the age. Is it exile, escape,
a public ceremony to honor him, prison, execution?

Don't be so anxious, the poem said, or you'll wake me up
before we get there. But how could I help it? Because
we kept on walking, walking, to my father's
jouncing stride, till I had recognized the movement,
could feel the rhythm of bedded lovers rising in me,
rising, I couldn't stop it, and here I am,
alone, wet with the riddle of the old realities.

REVISITING THE CONFESSIONAL AS A TOURIST

This is the place I used to lug my sins to
as if I carried the weight of my own absence.
The void was only a few holes then
but heavy enough already.

In whispers he told me to pray yet the poem heard him.
How could I help praying? After all, I began
bowed to my knees in the waters of the womb.

Rebaptizing Father, wash the death-smell
of your withering genitals off your fingers
and water me in the font of my own sorrow.
Then see how you make me grow.

I remember the poem told me: the real dark
is a door you can walk through
but can never open.

Outside, the wind whimpered like a beggar
asking no less of me than a life.
The poem stood so still it almost disappeared.

Sometimes, sleeping among the brutes,
I seem to remember when brain turned into mind
and the gods were born.

POEM ALMOST IN TIME FOR EASTER

(For John Matthias)

"Yesterday a man identified as Timothy Eastman was found stabbed to death in his apartment at 324 Lamont Avenue."

From a newspaper story,
Saturday, March 29, 1975

The poem arranged it for him. How else
could he be murdered on the very Friday
which has for centuries been called good?

For instance he hardly noticed that the door
he'd left behind him locked was now unlocked.
Yet the betrayer who stood inside in the shadows,
close enough for a friend's embrace, he knew at once.

He even recognized the knife, it glittered
with the sunlight of his mother's kitchen, it had
carved for years the warm meat of his birth.

The potted lily slipped from his hands,
he heard its roots suck at the floor.
The stab however was too sudden, he could not
believe until he'd stuck his hand in the wound.

Not in the flash that ripped the holy curtain
but in the darker light of thunder that lingered
on, he saw forming the one chance in his sixty years
to cry out, Nothing is finished! Nothing!

23

But then, as if to keep the secret, the poem
left his voice, and not even his patriarchs
came running from their graves to speak for him.

And so he knew it was he alone who was
surrendering, as each living thing at last
surrenders and no one is to blame.

It was he skulking down out of himself
by the back stairs, his legs melting, and he
seeping into the spring rain outside.

There, in blood as bland as water, he'll rinse
the soft bones of snow from street and avenue
to make way for saviors marching with their saints
and for demons pranking with their sinners.

THE POEM FAILS AT MICHEL'S, HAIRSTYLING FOR MEN

"But the very hairs of your head are all numbered."

The poem holds open the door to this parlor
of sorcery. You enter but protest at once
that all the magic has been scraped off.

The perfumes tainting the air are tinsel
ghosts, they could kill acres of flowers.
Bare numbers that have counted lives over
and over in those cushioned chairs in a row
spring up, clanking, in the cash register
like mounted skeletons.

But see, the poem insists, that man
sitting still as death in his high seat,
the mystic robe draped over his shoulders,
arms and lap. Watch him shut
his eyes, open them, stare dazed
at the empty space around his feet,
then close them again. Under the spell
of the shaman who stands beside him anointing
his head, the man dozes toward vistas.

Understand, it's the hair of the man's head
the medium is stirring his hands in,
it's a man's head, it's where nerves have gathered
from rock and leaf, from fish, bird and reptile,
all come home at last to play
sad, comic games.

25

And look—the poem points—that ring
on the necromancer's finger, weaving
in and out of the trance. It's flashing
signals toward a future here
already in the mirror. From his side
of the dream the man has not yet seen it
or he would seize the hand and kiss
the ring's meaning. But maybe he does see,
maybe he's hissing through the teeth
of his bowed head: kill, kill that serpent
coiled around your finger that writhes and sparkles
through the destinies hanging on my every hair.

2.
BODIES
CARVED IN FANTASY

ORGANON

Let me examine you, she said,
meaning my privacy.
Surprised but glad to oblige
exposure before a woman
I'd never seen before.

And as she pressed and peered
she defined our parts, mine
licensed amateur, hers professional
stretching the pride in bone of blood
another inch of miles.

Thank you, my dear, chaste kiss
on cheek, for something not paid for
by the dollars tucked in her garter.
Knowledge of body, was it, warm
as milk, and lost as in romances, lost.

Now you be sure and come back,
standing like a door in shadow
always ajar. And I've gone back
so many times I wonder if maybe
she's dead by now. Such opening
of the gates, such vigor of practised buttocks.

My books gaze down at my dog
licking himself. If we could reach
our organs and apertures like that
with our kissing, speaking, eating
mouths, my fellow immortals and I,
would our narrative be worse.

The organ pipes, I seem to remember,
reverberated in heroic chords.
Fat with refuse which those anthems
left behind, the rats of nightmare
roll out from below the pedals.

The keyboard locks, we watch
them waddle to the timbers
of our wistful heaven and gnaw.

DIANA AT LAKESIDE

She stands in tan-warm twilight, still
as the softskinned lake she's watching,
one knee casually bent,

as if those trim sun-seasoned legs
had not been grown to tangle
with a lover's legs, untangle,
then wrap him tightly in.

Her hair carved down to her shoulders
like a brown gold bell leaves not
a wisp for the wild wrestle
when mouth and hands storm, dishevel.

Who can stare hard enough
to help her feel a cushioned
lover ride the void where now
her lax arms embrace her breasts?

That wound of love that she was born with
sleeps too far beneath the obvious
bikini to be reopened.

Dig fingers and toes in sand, only
drag your glare off her. Her
concealments are easy and still,

as sunset-deep as the long water
she looks out on but not into.

31

ACTAEON TO ARTEMIS
IN THE AFTERLIFE OF THE ART GALLERY

"The work of hunters is another thing."

I tell you I never saw you naked.
It was out of fantasy your body carved
for me those supple erotic prayers.
Whatever nakedness there was, was you.

And so in the vengeance of your self-contempt
must my network of reveries harden
and load my head with antlers? Will you
thicken my fingers to caressing hooves?

I see small mercy in your tawny cheekbones,
I see I'll need both hands to pray with.
Consider these hounds of mine, ungainly,
dangle-eared, which I have feathered

like arrows to fly at desperate game,
will you goad them, then, on me
to slash my images of you like meat?
Here at the crossroads it is always night,

even at noonday, and only dreams
can decide. I wait for you to flower
in the full and not the dark moon of yourself.
But fingers already are coalescing,

brain sags heavy with horn. In the distance
which you keep always safe around you
are you leaning and listening toward
your satisfactory wails of hounds?

UNDONE, DOING

When he helped her carefully undo
her dress, she would not admit
of any but minor creatures scurrying,
would contend how kittens swirled
to hide their eyes in paws of small fur.

When he kissed, lightly of course,
each nakedness unleafing one by one
she still felt only in miniatures
as if to define a shrill of crickets
warming into nooks of an autumn house.

And she allowed gladly,
still in praise of little scamperings,
when he folded the whole body
of love (he called it) completely
over her, fantasy to foot.

She would have argued then
to remember the first-year squirrels,
that they circled grass and bark
and kept balance, twig to branch.
Her mind, bulging with body, fingered

the hard-shelled meats pouched in their jowls.
And some of these (as she lay playing)
she guessed the tiny claws would bury
and forget so that solemn-rooted trunks
might grow to the shade of hickory or of oak.

EVELYN IN THE APRIL SUN

At twelve years what she wears
allows not half an inch to
ignorance: sweater sharpens the
comedy of beginning breasts to
just a threat of seriousness,
buttocks rounded soft in
brightly flowered pants
parody anticipation so
narrowly they alarm.

When she walks, bell bottoms
ring announcements and no one laughs.

The noon light takes up with her, it
glints electric knowledge all
through her long carefully careless hair while
we stand darkened in our
privilege of years, able
only to know how easy it can
be to make her cry.

A WOMAN ABOUT TO BEGIN

Suddenly, to violate the gently dawning
hills and valleys of your body is everybody's
meaning. Remember, the knight himself
was the visored paramour of his lord's lady,
the confessor a cowled pander who whispered
between seducer and seduced. But how escape,
now the disguises are bold in print
and the real actors everywhere are clamoring?

Who taught you to be ready? Shadows
of complicity are busy behind your gaze.
Drowsing on your eyelash is the animal
you train in secret to devour all ravage
of fantasy and muscle, then wait serene
and still for the delicate pollen touch.

OLD-TIMER

What a creation he was, made
of old crimes and rags, his mouth
a smear of dirt, a clot of mud
for a heart. Yet words of his
made the boulders shudder for miles
and you could hear wings whistling
from the uncreated springtime
of everybody a child.

Terrified then (you heard them panting)
they tore at their horse's tail of his hair.
they dug at their hell holes in his eyes
until they found his infinitesimal
lightning bug of life and stamped it out.

They buried and buried him (his rags)
and never once could keep him in the ground.
How he seized for instance the basement
furnace for megaphone and whispered along
warm pipes into every room of the house.

He makes no sense, say the elders.
They shake heads in a row along their bench
of watery sunlight, they whittle the soft
blocks of their alphabet to look like testicles.

But the young men must willing sing all night
like dancing in magic circles of girls
whose thighs keep delicate time, keep time,
whose breasts almost hidden in the crackling
bushes of their long hair nod and nod to the sound.

PRIAPUS AT THE ADDING MACHINE

He has a head to stick in the fire
and from his tail two eggs are jouncing.
From this a dozen daughters may rise
to stand in snow, breathe soot from fog;
or ten sons, to choke on pills and wear
tin collars for prancing through beds of daisies.

Can the women count on fingers dipped
in the bubbling juices of desire? *Do* they
in fact count? Or do their men, for all
their deep voices, count? Billions of asterisks
too far removed in night to betray
their violence are blinking a frantic NO.

Why have the women's milky ovulations
brushed arcs of fury across the zodiacs,
their men slapping at stars like swarms of insects?
Just yesterday the mothers were counting love
by love in the countless leaves which bush
and tree lifted from star-shade into shapes of dawn.

WATCHMAN, WHAT OF THE NIGHT?

Do you think it has been my pleasure
keeping the night watch year by year,
clutching our common loneliness
to myself alone so you might sleep
in the busy logic of your days?

They are yours too, these difficult lords,
these imps and trolls and the deeper demons
of the long dark hours. And such unlikely
elves and angels as I've encountered
singing their loving mischief have sung

to unnerve the fatted flesh of your
unfaith as well as mine. Would you
believe to feel in our briny blood
the graze of scales where monsters rise
dripping, their alien stares a-leer,

their maws opening in search of us?
You complain of bad dreams but I
defend your dreams against the stench
of hairy beasts buried alive, God knows
how long, among our fathers' graves.

In the bad dream of the news you waken to
do you creep along the abyss of the moment
and hear the hollows in yourself echo
that first fierce stroke of nothingness?
I climb to our bedroom, my ears wild

with chatter of the countless dead against
the booming blood of silence. There
I wait for the dawn of children's voices
running barefoot away from dreams,
for then come tears of sleep to release me.

LOVE GAME

If other ways and kinds of
love fail, try this love-making:
make a poem and get you

lovers you'll never see or
know of, by thousands, hundreds or
three or two. Be sure you

get one lover though,
namely, yourself. Him you
knew only too well

yesterday but now he
shines unknown again and
lights up crowd on crowd that

may be there or not. You
may of course get none again.

3.
THE MANY
MOUTHS OF GOD

NEARING WINTER

Two pairs of mallards, tandem,
swim the pond in a soundless
march. The males in white collars
search through the dusk of rain,
their motives cold as silence,
their hens brown as November drizzle.

Of such adroit inconsequence,
which is easier to say:
that time stoops down from the affairs
of suns and planets, from the hush
of light-years, to become four feathers

balancing on an eyedrop,
or that this moment listens
to forgive an earth that shakes so
with savage important noise.

ORCHESTRA

O the times now that
God goes out of tune and
praise tames down to
such quaint anthems

even child catechumens ask each
other's eyes, Is this all that
fearsome parent was?

Or the music inflates
altogether out of control.
(At such times watch the
women.) The women

scream their clothes off and
with raped knives hack the
musician into pieces, they

slop his parts still smoking
into the stream. (Listen, in
pieces he welters fluting to the sea.)

MOUNTAINS

This quiet of mountains whispering to mountains could demand your
    complete disappearance in the most blatant sunlight.
Winds shake their heads, they'll have nothing to do with these trees,
    not even the tallest.

A road ancient as Abraham's cattle leads your fifty-miles-an-hour
    on and on and says nothing.
Although ear and eye may swivel in every primitive direction, they
    will not detect anything at all
because events happen here like unimaginable sculptures, neutral,
    to one side or the other of every place there is
and they keep no time small enough for clock-towers.

The stillness among mountains has no right whatever.
It may be only the subtlest bones in your own head vibrating.

SUDDENLY THIS LEFT-HANDED LIFE

Look out, we're about to knock something over, knuckles,
knees, elbows, shoulders, hips and feet
stick out in all at once gawky directions,
they bump objects the dusk warps out of place,
we feel them totter, we don't know what they are
except their blunders thud to the bone, familiar.

Our heads however graze tall things altogether
strange, they set them teetering like metronomes
that won't stop, we squeeze our blood small, they won't stop,
they keep on waving at us like hello or goody-bye.

POSTURE

He hammers his tambourine
against his ankles, "not abjectly,"
he says, "but serenely,

risking what my posture
may confess
that I don't know."

His look just shy of pride,
he bangs his rhythms
inside the dance,

he stoops among those bodies
vertical, aswirl, those
upright leapers, snatchers at stars.

The bones of his spirit
he bends down. "The many
mouths of God," he says,

"must breathe along this floor
where feet are twinkling."

MAY MORNING

The young wives trundle their baby-carriages
in the public sunshine of the park, confessing,
childlike, the sins they'd accuse the whores of.

They don't know yet how to wrap their infants
into the prescribed packages of mortality.
They haven't learned how to forgive love.

HIJACK

Picking up
speed
as if his
trouble
rose to
roar and
scream

he took off
from the runway
circled once
the peripheral
reality

then headed
straight
inside
himself

VIEWS OF OUR SPHERE

We deserved that earth-shot from the
moon's asbestos-gray horizon: a
family portrait on the old homestead, yet
not a single one of us could be
seen and the only history being made was
storm-swirls over rocks and oceans.

So our prophets from as long ago as the
close of paradise had at last a
picture to illustrate their remarks.

As the atoms in our invisible heads
go on blasting out toward darker and
darker lights what can we hope for but
smaller and smaller snapshots of this place
already small and lonesome enough.

The countdown, however, is pulsing in all our
engineered spaces of mind, and each flight
now must explode into the next till
we and our shape in the sun and our weather
vanish altogether (all together).

UP AIR

Don't you go out
there and get
lost. Yes ma'am.

Passenger by passenger
safety-buckled to the air
they rocket up.

Where we going, pardon
me, I mean where
we flying?

Don't know but I've
heard stories. So've I. So
why not,

they're telling stories.
You stay in here, hear?
we got places,

we keep hours, by
God you be in bed by
midnight.

How to watch clocks when
Thanksgiving at grandma's
is not a where

at all. Wherever, he says,
we're going, I've heard we won't
go all the way.

You can't go on thinking like
that, he says, try running a
bank like that,

try running a government.
Christmas, shut up, he
said, but I mean

look for July Four on the map,
everybody, he yells, look down
at the grand Canyon.

All right then, ask the
stewardess how far are
we from where?

Well, you might say from the
sun. That's no place to
start from because

I did mean when, we really
did mean where. So you're
trouble-makers,

never satisfied, she says
and camera, her cute ass waggles
down the aisle

like any street anywhere
and when they stretch their
legs, whenever.

FALL RAIN

Thunder, old man and
blind, grumbles from
corners. Old too is
rain that keeps falling,

weakly falling, yet
dissolves the roofs over
all you remember into
swamps again, it

will take the sun
centuries to dry them
back into nothing.

MEMORANDA:
from AGENT IN THE DARK
to CENTRAL INTELLIGENCE

Monday, Late Evening

Because you have buried dead people
whole for years, no ghosts
interrupt this surrounding dark.

Yet the soil is befouled with souls.
They seethe, angrily invisible,
in the ganglia and at the brain root.

Tuesday Noon

Airline passengers, thermometers
in mouth, rise to such stillnesses
they freeze beyond repair.

Darkened movie houses
and television rooms invite
suicides of ear and eye.

Saturday, Every Hour

One by one, swiftly
invented futures recede
into the present and are lost.

Sunday, 5:42 a.m.

These nights can't be slept in,
the days can't be wakened to.

YEAR

Autumn endured beyond rumor.
All around us groves of rainbows
kept promising.

Snow came finally and we were
quarreling with winter
for our lives.

Christmas trees kept falling
down, the sawed roots
slipped at last.

No houses burned, some decorations
broke, a few children knelt to scc
how empty these baubles were
inside.

Leaves will return in season
to their lofty perches,
they will inspect us, maybe
judge us.

IF BACK TO OLYMPUS

A lightning bolt of mud
flashes all windows black,
mountains splatter
into space to sound the thunder.

The father's hand that reaches
out toward us goes mad, gives
air to drink, water to breathe.
His lavas hiss and freeze us
into fossils out of time.

Icebergs with our meat
suspended in them tinkle
in his glass like laughter.
He drinks his nectar cold.

Imagine his succulent ambrosia.
Flesh of ours melts back upon
his tongue to when the reptiles
scrambled up from his salted seas.

This is the sacrament
of us he eats and drinks
by day, forgets, and again
by night consumes.

DESIGNS FOR SLEEP

My sleeping marrow rearranges
me again. For what watchers
in the dark do these bone-ends dipped in my blood
trace kaleidescopes of trunk
and branches, swivel-neck and crown?

They shift their contrivances of me
on a bed without edges. Although the shapes
breathe hard, I'm not yet bleeding out.
I stay inside all their changes of design.
Night by night I go in deeper.

RAINY DAY: JOGGING INDOORS

Helps me lift my feet high,
six-shooter tickling my heels.
"Dance, dance, if you want to live."
I do. I dance. Gunpowder
burns up the air I pant for.

Spatters the dust around my feet again. "Faster,
faster, live longer." Bullies the
crowd to laugh, me in my fear
running on old legs in one place.

Tired of the fun, will aim straight
at me, crack-shot and knows where. Will
where matter? because rest for me then
in one place, taste of my blood
cooling in bullet smoke.

SKEPTIC

I can't believe my hands.
I stare at them open-fingered.
They look like hands I've seen
hanging at the ends of old men,
shrunk into wrinkles, veins distended
like gray blood choking.

When my morning goddess
got me my long youth,
why didn't she also
ask to make me immortal?

MASTER OF CEREMONY

Let everyone, he announces, speak a minim
below his understanding and yet be understood.
What else, he asks, are words for?

Divide, he tells us, that space between cloud
and hill by the snow that unfolds down all night.
In what's left over will there be room for the blind
prophet you thought you glimpsed
snowshoeing through an Arctic fury?

Or multiply, he says, the time from thunder
down to valley by speed of rain pelting
the lake-skin to a fur of mist. Will you
that way magnify shorelines to seduce the deaf
singer sloshing barefoot through the rain forest?

Better could we learn, in school or out, he preaches,
how to evade the luxury of sorrow or cure
addictive ecstasies of pain. It's how to shove
the little by little words over the crag
of no statement, no question, as if

you swept the monsoon rain into rivers
or shoveled blizzards into oceans. Isn't it,
he asks, only below the muscular contention,
below the stretching tight of nerves
where love lives real, down, down?

WHAT TO DO AT THE END

There ought to be something quick
to make a life nearing done
appear.

Maybe a maul to crumble
the slag away in one stroke
and release

a dance in granite. Or,
a veil to whip off so I
can see,

and without my antique face on
my daughter's eyes, can say
to her, look.

Hurry, my son is talking
statements, statements, and I hear
nothing

but questions. Like doves they brush
the window with leafing twigs
pilfered

to foretell his years still deep
in the tide. What to do with
lives

that begin and end shaped
like water. Here I am
my boy,

can you see me my girl.
All I say is quick quick
and like

any drowning child I can
only tell quick means
alive.

LONE

When the electric lights went out
and candles refused to burn
and there were no more matches,

he went on drinking wine in the dark.
It was how he conceded his complicity
in the loss of light, with no confessor near him

to witness, interrupt, or forgive.

MOMENT

The impotent man answered, 'Sir, I have no man when
the water is troubled, to put me into the pool.'

The healing is once only
or not at all, the moment of forever
caged in my kneeling bones.

The people are chanting holy, holy,
around it, the celebrant holds up to it
the disc of bread, saints in the windows
stand painted motionless for it.

Here in my folded palms my stone
melts into me the real name
of who I am and need not ever again
try to be. I have never been away.

My journeys are distances
and times swirling around me.
I will never have to explain.

Belief is me. I have room now
to live in all my doubts.
(There must be joy, that leisure of joy.)

Our gods, human and ghostly, female
and male, have suffered much already
for all of us. Will they rejoice to suffer me
into myself which being past is about to come?

4.
KINDRED FROM AS FAR AWAY AS HOME

FATHER FAMILIAR

Gnarled tobacco chewer,
sweated around the yard
and spat copiously into
my mother's bed of
old-fashioned flowers.

So I became in February
and soon after became two eyes
to keep watch on his one
hand could strike in a single
stroke my two ears deaf.

And then grew both soft
nostrils also for nothing but
to record in this world
the sour-sweet of his sweat,
like alcohol, I swore later,

drinking hard for him,
for all that violence in the flowers,
because never took one drink in
all his life the neighbors
shaking their heads behind curtains.

Ten years on and hear me
saying, I'm saying for God's sake
don't die yet, I'm no farther than
those dripping petals in spring,
looking down on his bed,

71

you can't die yet, you've
got to clean me of the guilt I
still accuse you of, something
has to be said, even written
down, or all that war of

years between us is lost.
But died in his anger
nevertheless. Peace, the nun-
nurse, peace now. But who could
know his fury if I did not

so stooped to kiss and
sure enough the delicate
sweet-sour of his to the last.

DAY IN JUNE

I was stretched out in my aluminum lawn chair
gazing up at the maple tree that shaded
my car in the driveway, not listening
to our kids playing with the kids
in the next yard, yet hearing them.

I was not dreaming but not quite thinking either
how I'd have to call for an appointment soon
to have my car checked over—carburetor, plugs,
distributor points, and especially that battery
now three, or was it four years old, remembering
like a footnote I hadn't even had the snowtires changed.

Gradually I began to see what I'd been staring at
for several minutes or it seemed it might be for several years:
the whole mass of maple leaves moving in the easy
rising and subsiding wind. When I closed my eyes
I could feel the wind like watching a woman walk alone
in an open field raising and lowering her eyes
and turning her head slightly to this side and that side
as it suits her, who doesn't know she is being watched
and wouldn't care if she did know, through one long
summer afternoon that might be lasting forever.

The leaves, when I opened my eyes, were a different motion, though.
They complicated the wind with contradictions.
Near the top, in the center, there were leaves fluttering
like rapidly shaken bells and they went on vibrating
even when the wind had seemed to die. Lower down,

the leaves suddenly lolled on the solemn nod of a branch
and then as suddenly went back to sleep.
On another branch the leaves were going around, around
in gestures as profoundly mechanical as grieving.

Then without warning, like a dream that explodes noiseless into
    thought,
here they all were, all of them, leaf by leaf, dancing together
    in one dance.
And the one act of sight that took them in required my whole life
and more, and I felt myself sinking, pleasantly drowning from
    hair to toenail
in the tides of salt blood that the muscles of the heart learned
    long ago
from what the revolving moon, long before that, had taught the sea.

There I was in the one act of seeing and breathing, being danced
    by the maple leaves,
driving my car to the office and back, day after day,
the earth twirling the days to each other through moons of the
    seasons,
and I was dancing the dance of love with my wife between moons
and sitting with her at the table after dinner going over the
    monthly bills
until I heard the voices of children in the next yard piping to
    the same dance.

Then it was over. I had not drowned in my own blood, in the
    knowledge of it.

I was sitting in my lawn chair gazing up at the maple tree.
It was then, I suppose, the thinking began but still in a kind
    of dream.
Suppose, I thought, we bring in our most advanced techniques
and concentrate them on this tree in the wind, calculate to a
    hair
the flexibility of stems, the tensions and torsions of boughs,
measure the weights of twigs, the force of the wind, its delicate
    shifts of direction,
its subtle accelerations and subsidences. And then suppose we pour
the organized question of our data into the most sophisticated
    computer
we can fabricate and wait for its answer.

Suppose further that we (turning gradually into they)
call up an imagined head mathematician by long distance code
    number
and ask him to provide an isomorphism from his stock
of models, and suppose, then, they finally arrive at the law
of the leaves' complex motion in the June wind.

I who began as witness, now must rise defendant and hear their
    verdict.
Suppose they judge me the victim of pure delusion,
the dance being not in the tree but on my nerve-ends.
Dragged off to their dungeon of oblivion
I can at least kneel there and give bitter thanks
for my moment of seeing which they having sight
beyond their eyes are blind to, lest they should see. Or suppose
they let me go until their brothers, the analyzed analysts

75

of the brain, arrive in court a few years later
and decide whether I saw or merely dreamed out
some deeply sleeping wish.

But suppose they say, you were right, our hypothesized data
confirm your surmise. This acquittal is the doom I fear the
          most.
Think of the terrible freedom—to live your whole life through,
hearing the conscience of your vision beating out
loveless numbers for leaves and tides and hearts to dance to.

O my children, sons and daughters of this convicted felon,
you pipe now to the dance which you think is play
but you will have to learn better than he has learned
how to poise your years on the ever finer edge,
having to doubt all things for your minds' sake
yet having to believe for your very breath.

IN PURSUIT

Gaited to old short fatted
bones of legs, room
to room, upstairs, down,

spins panting, flicks off light
by light behind tall children
(their sunburned marble smiles).

How hands tremble damp
afraid, expense left burning
from space to space where no one

is, five lamps grin
in TV room alone,
pictures talking, no one

left to listen, kitchen
then where no one cooks,
table, no one eating.

Spins, cocktail, damn it,
drools rug to rug, what of it,
through door by door, hurry,

no time left for balance,
children bland by face
flip switches on, blaze trails.

Follows, helpless, hopeless,
darkens, saves, because
not ever life enough

to burn from, how he knows,
how they can't feel it, tall
and smile like statues, as

for instance, this house blazing,
every light left on.

LIGHT AS A QUALITY OF MERCY

I

At the end of each short winter day
the dark entered the kitchen
just as the milk came in warm
from the barn. And grandma lighted a lamp

as for some hulking gentle
stranger who had travelled far,
was tired and had little to say.

II

From Elaine's cupped hand a baby
light is born at the candle tip
and you can see its delicate breathing
making friends of the faces around the room.

III

The switches flip, one—TWO—three—FOUR,
and light leaps out hard as guns
to occupy precisely the oblong room.

79

GROWING INTO LIGHT

What can you prophesy, you wonder,
of this child who laughs in her sleep night
after night, hugging her jokes to herself
in the privacy of dream

What cost, you wonder, may the sun exact
for such secret levity when it warms its own
unpredictable dreams into hard being
and she will have to call it a day, Amen.

CELEBRANTS

Who'll drink the dead man's whiskey? Don't
all swear at once. Give us time
to count his faithful and their years.

Aunt Karen says besides a quart one
quarter gone he left two more
he'd never touched. Oh hadn't he.

Unscrewed for us the bottle tops
like clowns' hats, his laugh gurgled
in our glasses, we heard it, didn't we.

Drank him for hours and drank again,
maybe by much raising of arms to hurrah
our way to where he lasts forever.

Because he was a miniature, wasn't he?
of the big all-God who got his feet
on the ground at last and when of course

we killed him levitated into rumors
of peace, peace (and war) repeated
around the earth two thousand years.

So Uncle Emil's blood amber-live
melted all the ice cubes we could
freeze. Yet how somber he glowed

lifted to our mouths for light,
for once not drunk, but being drunk,
and for the first time not good company.

THE WAY DOWN

She was able to kill herself.
She had the strength
and she dared.
But then her hands being dead
could not bury her.
That harder thing to do
she left to us.
It's what we're doing here
this morning.
We may never get it done.

NEIGHBOR: FOR TWENTY YEARS

I've watched the male strut of her female hips
crossing and recrossing the grass, her arms
yanking hose and sprinkler to always new
dry places. I've felt her blast through summer

like sirens, back door to garage, elbows
bent and arms swinging a stiff six inches
from her body, from shoulders sore with pride.
I confess to her laughter as a habit of my hearing,
she-voiced, crowing raucously over
the neighborhood.

                      This morning tree surgeons
have been felling the willow in the side yard.
Arms folded, she stands presiding over
a log just drawn from the trunk. Quickly
she stoops from round tight buttocks and with flat
of hand spanks the exposed raw white
of wood, slap slap.

MEETING

Don't I know you? Weren't we young once?
Our lithe breaths walked in sentences, I believe,
along miles of country roads, not tiring.
And afterwards we swilled them with beer
like insatiable pigs all night.

Easy, we thought, in sweat of words to talk
our lives-long into shapes that we could love
or at least endure: we were shameless
rubbing our naked wishes against each other.

Now our faces fumble with barely audible
greetings and we turn away. For we have both
been lived by others. At every strategic crossing
those engineers, heads bulging in helmets,
pointed thick fingers at maps saying,
the road will run here. And it did.

SOON, LIKE RIGHT NOW

Poem for a Homecoming

Eftsoons, the poem says,
not even needing to smile,
knowing perfectly well what it's saying,
eftsoons the universe (as you know it)
drops all hands-up and becomes serious.
Already marsupials are invading
paved tundras of the ordinary.

There's an old knowledge, the poem says,
mortared into walls that's thicker
than art. After all, Einstein
elbows out into air, doesn't he?
And hear the salt fisherman
crying, "Kaleidescope, kaleidescope!"
Mountains, believe me, are not lofty

for nothing. Coming home from England
my poet thought he stumbled
on every wave, Greek Neptune
speaking nothing now but the gruffest Anglo-Saxon.

THOSE ELDERS OF THE GREAT TRADITION
&
THE REST OF US

It's as if they dreamed their knowledge
and what they dreamed is what we know.
Who can blame them? They could hardly
have believed this sequel to themselves,
that all their wisdom is really happening.

Yet how can we endure these great grandfathers
of the best we know, who still must sit on every
committee of our thought, who interrupt
our counsels with their wise irrelevancies?
They take their time too, having at their leisure
all history while for us the hour is real.

DOG DRINKING AT NIGHT

In the darkened house he drinks
and drinks me gradually awake
to a new rhythm happening to water.

Like a fountain at first,
glittering on the ear.
But no—darker, closer to earth,

thirst of tongue that keeps
time to what it thirsts for,
liquid beat, cadence

salted away in the blood.

And dog and man pulsate
to primal wonder like fin and wing
whenever what is needed, is.

MAIL FROM HOME IN THE SKY

Cozy above us a little airplane chugs
along, all in white. It feels like a pet bird
that knows its home, a throb of our neighborhood
warm in the sky.

                      We watch it turn to slow
pastel pink, surprised yet not surprised.
(Have we, then, begun to remember?) Its toy
motor stills, only our blood thumps the air.

It curves its homespun wings, it's looking
down for a place to fall to and be sick in,
decides with a sudden dip and plunges.
Listening for the crash we grow back down
to children, smaller, smaller, hands pressed hard
but not too hard against ears. When it sounds,
the crash is fur and cotton, we have to hunt
it down past corners limp as water, our legs
are as young as fins.

                    And Mr. D'Arcy's roof
is not caved in, the Hornbacks' garden is not
in ruins. The wreckage lies content among
junked cars in Mr. Garcia's lot next
to the tracks. Fuselage, wings and tail
have crumbled off like sunset, only the tiny
motor grins, intact and dead.

No flame or smoke. The pilot's body has slid
down the smell of hot oil and grease to nothing.
Policemen dressed as important people are poking
looks like x-rays at everything and everybody.
But what can *they* do? Indoors at home we know
that what has happened can't unhappen, ever.

THE CRICKET SOUND

Trucks bull down the highway,
double wheels bellow, shake the ground.
Overhead jet-liners howl,
scream low to housetops

yet the September insect din,
thin in the grass as time,
skilled as time, shrills through.

Acres of diminutive telephones
call us from under grass. They ring,
ring, wave on wave, harmonize, clash.

Those crowds, those fathers of ours
have thought of urgent things
they forgot to tell us. Or they've relented.

Or repented. They ring and ring to us
from under grass. Even those first
erect near-men, millions of years
away, have something frantic to say.

They won't get through our hard noisy heads.
Already before snow stills the grass
we are listening as dead to them
as they ring dead to us.

NEAREST OF KIN

Lucky isn't it that
people
        when they
die
   can't go on
walking around or
talking but

          have to
lie down
          have to be very
still and
          have to be
still
all the time

          because
that way
       we
notice
them

TO FRANK O'MALLEY
(1908–1974)

What have you done? You lie so still
you strain belief in our mortality.
We can't believe the body of your ghost,
lithe and fleet, has now been exorcised.

Our scholar gypsy, you haunted the conscience
of all our paths and corridors,
you sharpened with light the shadow that was cast
on what we yearned for in dome and spire.

You christened writers of indiscreetly
visionary words, the baptized
and unbaptized alike, while awed
multitudes of the young looked on.

You gospelled four decades of rich and poor men's
sons showing them where the soul is.
And each day you knotted them thongs to whip
the money-changers from the temple door.

When did you first surmise that yours
must be the gift of loneliness?
When did you discover that he
who is loved by all is loved by no one?

Foreknowing, as you did, such cost of spirit
how did you decide? Or did you?
How can a man, a mere man, decide
to make nothing but himself his own.

There were days we scarcely could endure
the fury of that indifferent love
that smiled or glowered in your eyes.

Forgive us if we found it hard
to quite forgive in you your relentless
understanding of yourself.

But we salute you now as then
with love, across no greater distance
than you always kept, immaculate
and warm, between yourself and us.

CHILDREN LYING IN THE DAZED HEAPS OF THEIR BONES

1.
I put the gun of their hunger
to my skull but can't pull
the trigger. My wife's in the kitchen.

2.
In our neighborhood bar a Judge,
a Congressman, or President
foams in every beer.
A General sniffs each glass of wine.
Drink up. Let's go home to dinner.

3.
These old people on television
starving into little bodies
restore us to kindergarten.
We finger our ABC's
waiting like tiger cubs for lunch.

4.
Farmers, listen to your fields
of amber grain tumble into cocktail
lounges in cascades of clinking glasses.

5.
While we were blind with infancy
mother put in our mouths
the cow's tit for her own.

And see how we grew and grew,
sons and daughters of cattle
in the dung-warm barns.

6.
Out here in the open meadow
the tons of beef and lamb
masticated into my tenderly
rounded body begin to low
and bleat against an angry sunset.

7.
Sharp sips of coffee by candlelight
carve the pastry in our mouths
into figures of contemplation.
We chew like monks under rule of silence.

"A LITTLE FOLDING OF THE HANDS TO SLEEP"

An old man's sleep is never done.
Every winter night he carefully
stretches his shallow dreams across many wakings.

He hoards all the little yawning times
of days for naps, he saves the pauses
in conversation toward almost imperceptible dozes.

It is never enough.

Those were nights when all night long
the skins of love rubbed fire
from each other like repeated dawns
and sleep was beyond question squandered.

The baby however kept warm for only
two hours in the hospital incubator.
For that brief kick and cry in unshaped
light, din of sounds, sting of touches,
he's been sleeping for fifty-two years.

He still sleeps.

POEM MADE OUT OF QUESTIONS

An old woman in a far off country
washing clothes on stones in a little stream
may do the prayer that keeps breath in your body.

And no doubt many old women in wheelchairs
have never been born. But until you can touch fire
and feel only the light, how can you know?

Experts with badges shining on their hearts
are hunting a man whose passion left a girl
dead in the ditch of last night's news.

They train their dogs and lights on his trail,
they search frantically as for hidden treasure,
for the girl's father weeps and curses in his need.

Will he write for her, ever, this epitaph:
love your killer as yourself?

The time for breathing is brief. And you need
years to rehearse hurting before you're ready.
The end of you which you puzzle over and resist,

will that be, then, the reward, a forced
surrender to the imagination of love?

NARCISSUS FLOWERING

We are riveted and
hinged upon ourself in
such oblique directions

(so many, and not foreseen)

how can you tell
what will happen?

Every day, it could be, you
find an uncle cozy in a
cranny of your blood swishing his

fist of beer almost in
your eye.

Or at table where your
bone crooks into elbow is
sudden room for dozens,

it may be aunts, grandmothers,
who bring coffee rounding to snug aroma.

Consider too how love can
stoop as in those fairy
tales, how we almost say it,

almost on all fours: o lost
brother dog, o sister kitten.

Or at dawn a gauze of
snow smooth over grass, bushes,
trees, exposes such

familiars we are
ready to welcome cousins.

What father, or is it mother,
may focus from an unsuspected
color of our hair or eyes and

claim you then at the ultimate
connection or disconnection.

Date Due

APR 30 1983			

BRODART   CAT. NO. 23 233   PRINTED IN U.S.A.